THE SUN POEMS

GREG BACHAR

Books By Greg Bachar

Curiosisosity
2013

The Amusement Park of The Mind
(Essays On Thought, Feeling, Experience)
2013

The Writing Machine
(Writings On Writing: Occasional Ruminations
On An Intangible Legerdemain)
2013

The Book of Was
2016

THE SUN POEMS

GREG BACHAR

ROWHOUSE PRESS 2016

Cover Art by Derrick Buisch
Sun, Oil On Canvas 16" x 24" (2015)

ISBN # 9780971986770

THE SUN POEMS

THE SUN POEMS

SUNAWAY

Sunlight flows
honey woes.

Sunlight knows
what nobody knows.

Nobody knows
what sunlight knows.

There were times of day
the sun went away.

There were dogs at bay
that snapped sunshine away.

There were elephants in clay
that had sunshine their way.

There was that one day
my sunshine went away.

WHAT THE SUN KNOWS

Flares burn,
sunspots turn,
rays churn,
moons yearn,
ashes urn,
dolphins learn,
blooms fern,
darkness stern,
Mercury Saturn,
planets pattern,
asteroids return,
stars spurn,
rain cistern,
people sunburn,
dogs urine.

CORONAL EJECTION

Cellular corona,
solar granules,
sun as music,
sun as vibration.

Light – Foam
Light – Foam

Coronal undulation,
the sun's lyric,
energy modules,
see to listen.

SUN FATIGUE

The confusion
of always bright,
never knowing
the concept of night.

Always battling
the ice of space,
never dancing
in a cool embrace.

To never sleep,
never dream,
only roil an eternal beam,
its light too bright
to see that it is seen.

THE SUN'S ELIXIR

A cup of shade,
aubade jade. Smooth
out the web fantastic
with a crevice wink
while staying cool
at the ice-skating rink.
No glass of water,
no beads of sweat
to relieve the effort
of shining, no, OUTshining
the universe while
drunk on its own light.

SUN WRITER

The only book
that can save
your life is the one
you write yourself.

HUMIDITY

Sun spit,
a hummingbird dart,
tree sap,
orgy of deserts.

Halfway to the
barometer of desire
there are no
scales to follow.

The music is disjointed.
Stars splash into the lake of space.
Starfish slide upstream
towards the ray of beast,
the ray of quease,
the ray of ease,
come to fit
uncomfortingly.

EVEN THE SUN WILL DIE

Even the sun will die,
but not today.

A man sits patiently
in a wheelchair
outside the hospital
waiting for his ride.

The sun shines above
and casts the man's shadow
on the ground.

One day the man
will slip beneath his shadow,
one day the man
will slip beneath the ground,
but like the sun—
not today.

SHADOW CASTER

The sun delights
in casting shadows.
With a telescope,
it studies its craft.

"Oh, a good one,"
it thinks, and:
"Oh, a long one,"
it thinks, and
"look at that,
some move around
while some stay put
and shape shift
on the ground."

It is always day for the sun.
Perhaps its shadow craft is
performed out of envy of
those who experience night.

SUN TREES

The trees shake
their fist branches skyward
at the taunting sun
they so desire.

Asleep in their nest of night,
they dream of kissing sunlight,
out of reach but always in sight.

Every tree a member of
the sun's royal court,
and we their scribes
writing on sheets of their flesh—
sacrificed in rebellion
and easily sun burnt.

SHADE

In the shade of
a stand of birch trees,
a robin dawdles
for worms in the grass.

How can it hear
worms over the
thunder of the sun?

I have to huddle
in a building's shade
to write these lines
lest the sunshine
warp my mind.

Maybe it isn't listening
to worms.
Maybe it's listening
to shade.

LOST IN ITSELF (SUNDAY)

Despite never
taking a day off,
despite never knowing
the difference between
day and night,
the sun relaxed
and enjoyed its
Sunday.

SUNPLOSION

The sun, at some point
in its long formation
when there may have
been some belief in
becoming a moon,
before realizing
one day—another long
one—that it would
never escape itself,
that it would always
churn and never repose—
vowed to rage harder
and threw its fury far
and wide, unaware
that even its colossal light
would not reach somewheres.

SUN DIARY (EXCERPT)

Hot again today.
<u>Really</u> hot today.
Hot.
Hotter than yesterday.
Seems hotter than usual.
Record heat today.
Even in the shade it's hot.
Hot enough for ya?
The weatherman was <u>wrong</u>.
Air conditioner broke.
It's like a sauna in here.
The heat is on.

SUN TEA

Lemongrass had to have
been given its name
after both lemons and
grass were given
theirs, but surely it
was a known commodity
before. I like to think it
was known simply as
Sun Tea, as this is surely
the straw sweet root
the sun would steep to sip
in the middle of an especially
hot millennium—on ice.

SUNOUVENIR

In the center of the
sun, there's a little
room where it keeps
its bric a brac and
souvenirs from its
imaginary travels:
snail shells, witch hazel,
squirrel tails, blackberry
seeds, umbrella toothpicks,
the coaster from that bar
on that beach where
it sat and watched
itself set that time.

SUNDAY

The sun sighed and
withdrew into itself.
It didn't feel like
doing much but laying
around and staring into
space. It had been a long
stretch of days and
there was only a long
stretch of days ahead.
For just a moment, it
closed its eyes and almost
drifted off before it
caught itself, exhaled,
and sent a pulse
of itself into the universe.

SUNIZEN OF THE WORLD

"You're so galaxy,"
the sun thought, looking
at itself in the mirror.
It ruled all the planets
in the neighborhood
and all their moons too.
It ruled over the
asteroids and meteors
that passed through,
and the satellites and
probes and craft, except
perhaps, the ships from
other galaxies that made
it feel just a little less
galaxy when they passed.

THE NAKED SUN

Everyone is naked
beneath their clothes,
even the sun. Dressed
in rays, flares, spots,
and pure light, the
sun's clothes are the
same as what it wears
underneath. The sun
dresses itself in what
it is already wearing.
It is a naked sun
that shines down on us
even when fully dressed.

BEACH CLUB

The sun looked up
and down the beach,
surveying its length
to see who was under
all of the umbrellas.

There was Mercury, there
was Earth, there was Mars,
Saturn, Venus, Jupiter, Uranus,
Neptune and Pluto, all surrounded
by their moons and satellites.

The sun felt out of place.
No one looked its way.
No one spoke.

"Am I the only weirdo here?"
it thought, yearning for
a shooting star to cross
its path and stop.

SUN DOVE

The sun stared out
at the vast of its
expanse. Where was
love? Far away, but
how far? As far as the
Earth's moon? Farther?
It had to be as far as the
nearest star, and farther
if that star was not love.
Maybe that one? Or that one.
Or… But even the closest star
was too far with all that space
between. How to get to love?
And what celestial body was
brave enough to embrace
the sun? Only a black hole.
And who, the sun thought,
could love a black hole?

SUN THEMES

The infinite,
solar longevity,
illumination, magni-
tudinal longing, vicissi-
tudes of entanglement,
temporal resonance, the
shadow realm, synthesis,
incandescence, fluo-
rescence, seasonal ebbs
and flows, chandelier
thinking, flared ex-
pansion, ornithological
blindness, orbital
conjugations, bliss.

SUN CHANT

I am a fist and ball of flame.
No two days are one and the same.

I am a fist and ball of flame.
Bubble and roil and foil insane.

I am a fist and ball of flame.
Nothing comes between me and the rain.

I am a fist and ball of flame.
Nothing outshines the night of my day.

I am a fist and ball of flame.
I like to play, I like to play, I like to play.

THE SUN IS THE MOON

The sun is the moon,
they spoon, they spoon.

The sun is a funny cartoon,
of ruin, of ruin.

The sun's out of tune,
but croons, but croons.

The sun rides a flume,
and swoons, and swoons.

The moon loves the sun,
but runs, but runs.

The moon slips and falls,
that's not all, that's not all.

The moon is stuck in tides,
and doesn't arrive, doesn't arrive.

What's the sun to do,
but moo, but moo.

SUNDEITY

Sun worshipers gathered
at the shore for the
ritual. Sun worshipers
gathered on the mountain-
top. Sun worshipers gathered
in the desert. Sun worship-
ers gathered all over the
world to bow and make vows.
The Earth felt the vibration
of their chants and shivered
in ecstasy. The sun went
about its business, oblivious,
blinded to its followers
by its own light.

SUNCOMPLETE

The sun, shining and
bathing in its glory,
felt unfinished, felt…new,
a first time star
lacking the knowledge
and wisdom of its ancestors'
cosmic dawn cluster. Every
day was a new day—and there
was only one long, endless day,
always unendingly the same
as the last, or rather, itself.
How would it ever learn, it
wondered, if there was
only day and never night?

THE RAIN & THE SUN

Rain rains rainfall
war against the ground.

Sun beats down,
sun beats down.

Rain rains rainfall
sleep on dozy eyes.

Sun looks away,
sun looks away.

Rain rains rainfall
flood and breaks the dam.

Sun sees a lake,
sun sees a lake.

Rain tunes the Earth.
Sun just strums along.

THE SUN & THE RAIN & THE MOON

The sun's a jet set lounge
inside a merry-go-round.

The rain never stays but
comes and goes away.

The moon is blue because
it doesn't know what to do.

SUNSHIP

The sun runs aground
when bad weather comes around.

The rain makes us forget
that the sun never gets wet.

The rain ties a knot
and bobs along the dock.

The sun's a mystery won
after spring comes to knock.

The rain's a rusty key
that shuts the balcony.

The sun's a pesky flea,
that itches you, itches me.

The rain's a bloated mope,
the sun's a telescope.

The sun sets us free,
the rain is two for tea.

SUN-THIRTY O'CLOCK

The sun skips a knot,
prefers to roll unlocked.

Its shirt unbuttons a lot
to make the bathers flock.

The sun's a woozy dew.
What's a dark cloud to do?

There's no room in this town
for a moon that's upside down.

The sky's a lemon pie,
yellow and high.

The clouds are baked meringue,
come to harangue.

The moon's a cuckoo clock
on a Jell-o shot.

SUNWELL

The sun, nearing the end of
its days, began to flicker
and fade, but was still a
formidable foe for the
darkness being made.
Only now, in its faded
umbrage, did it see clearly
the celestial bodies it might
have called friends had
they not darkened and died
themselves, now all empty
shells of their previous
former selves. The sun shed
a tear that turned to steam
before it fell and disappeared,
its remaining heat still strong
enough to feel but show no fear.

THE SUN BALLOON

The sun balloon popped
into a sun drop and fell
atop a cloptropped fop,
its tear dropped mop a
warranted slop of
herringbone pop pop.
The prop shop's top cop
mopped up the chop shop
while slobbering romp
swamps bogged against
stomp stomps.   The sun,
ever prompt, rose atop the
morning's mountaintop,
while on its other slot,
it set beneath the sump pump.

SUNSIGHT

Perhaps solar flares are
the sun's way of seeing.
Blinded by its own light,
it throws a solar eye
out of itself to cast
a raygaze towards
its nearest realms and
beyond. Perhaps this is the
sun's only way of understanding
what those who don't possess
its seemingly infinite light
understand, and so now it too
knows from the flare of its gaze
that from the spark of first light
everything fades.

HUM SUN

The sun whispered:
I am a supernova.
I am a supernova.

And then the sun spoke:
I am a supernova.
I am a supernova.

And then the sun shouted:
I am a supernova!
I am a supernova!

And then the galaxy,
reflecting the sun's light,
took up the chant.

THE SUN IS INSANE

The sun is insane,
a renegade brain,
drained of all sane,
its rays a misty rain
machine gun enflamed,
too bored to refrain,
too wild to be tame,
too weird to be plain.
The moon's not to blame
for what the sun became.
Solar dust is its bane
when it tries to explain
why it stays in the game
day after day after day.

SUNROYALTY

The sun is Ruler
of the Shining
Everything, including
the moon, its swooning
buffoon. The moon is
Prince of the Low
Tide Kiss, especially
at risk if Princess
Asteroid doesn't miss.
The sun's The King and
Queen of Everything in
Between. Its royal court
is the solar system's
consort. The moon is wise
but knows nothing
without sunrise.

SUNBEAM

The sun's not welcome
in the night, its only
enemy save the fading
of its light. The night
is a maul of villagers
carrying torches like
clubs to batter the day
and keep its light at bay.
How long ago it was
that night and day got
along, but then like now
it was a moment fleeting
and brusk—light and dark
only mix briefly, once at dawn
and once at dusk.

RESUNS

What's the sun waiting
for? It spends an awful
lot of time in that part of
the sky. Why? If we weren't
here to absorb its light,
what would be its purpose?
To illuminate the empty
shelves of the planets in
this part of the universe?
What is its why? We know
what it does but not why it
does it. Why, sun, why?

LITERARY SUN

Unbeknownst to it, the
sun's an object of much
literary supposition,
the books it's in subject
to combustion were they
to near its margin.
It's not a well-read sun
despite all we've written.
It would require a sun-
proof book and a way to
get it into the sun's maws,
but even then would it want
to read our pondering
of its laws, or kitten stories
and puppy dogs?

SUNRISESETSUNSETRISE

The sunset is a sunrise
is a sunset is a sunrise.
The sun sets to rise and
rises to set. A sunset
here is a sunrise there.
A sunrise there is a sunset
here. The sun only sets
in places where it rises.
The sun only rises in places
where it sets. The sun
never sets or rises from
itself. The sun never sets
in the shade of a patio
umbrella eating a taco.
The sun never sits in the
shade next to a bench
writing poems about itself.

SUNSPHERE

The sun sets
to rise
and rises
to set.

The sun is
a doppelganger
in a corset.

The sun is
a little fish
in a petri dish.

The sun is
a golden eye
that never cries.

The sun is
not a meteor,
and neither
am I.

SUN TREE HILL

The sun sets on a little tree
upon the side of the hill.

The sunset doesn't worry me
nor the moon it tries to kill.

The sun is but a little frog
that doesn't know how to cry.

The moon is the best friend of fog
that covers up the sky.

I trust the moon though it
doesn't know what to do,

when, like the sun, the sky
has run out of the color blue.

SUNDAIRY

The sun's a little buttercup,
a plate of rolls about to
erupt. The sun's a cracked plate
of lust that does not slake
its thirst for thrusts. The sun's
a stream of butter cupped
to hear the spill of its
own voice. The buttered roll,
now buttered still, dabs tears
from the sun's eye, despite
the fact it doesn't cry
because butter isn't dry.

MOONSUN

The moon is just a ruin of dust,
a bag of spoons and sunset rust.

The sun plays tricks
with the moon's asterisk.

The moon hides its dark side
from the sun's hijinks.

The sun will never know
things the moon might have shown.

Like just how low the sunlight goes
behind the rise of the moon's glow.

Because the sun is always bright,
it never learns about moonlight.

The sun is devil of magma and pus.
The moon is angel of craters and crust.

SUNSPOT

We are a bunch of tiny dots
searching for our treasure spots.

The sun is one of the big shots
too big to fit in the coin slots.

It casts our shadows on the lot
while we cross and shout a lot.

Food left in the sun, it rots,
as do our dreams and tater tots.

We gave the moon a space shot,
but the sun is just a bit too hot.

And so we ground our dreams in pots
and shoot them down with slingshots

while the moon surrounds its pocks
with waving flags and astronaut socks.

ONE SUN

There's just one sun,
but I've seen more than one
while writing on the run
from shadows thrown
across the strum
of music played above the din
of summer heat and bobby pins,
the prick of which can sting and hurt
when one is singing in the dirt
as all the spheres go round
and round, the funhouse mirror sun
its loss, but every day our found.

THE SILVER SUN

The silver sun is a
ray-haired sun, its
tinsel bangs are
artist pangs as summer
fades to autumn. The
silver sun is a moonlit
sun, its reflection wavers
in Tranquility's craters.
The silver sun is a
setting sun, its goal
is the horizon. The
metal sun that melts and
runs to flow again next
season, the silver sun is
a friendly sun, one step
removed from gold, its
setting days and rising ways,
a morning that never gets old.

ORGY OF LIGHT

The sun writhes with other stars
in fleeting spasms of glory,
eons long as they thrust along
towards Destination Orgy.

Moons stand by as they
let out cries of ecstasy and agony.
Moons don't know what star throes
know and hang there without pageantry.

It's the sun and stars both near and far
that reap the most from writhing,
their lightning deeds and sunflower seeds
that rise and bloom come morning.

TRANSUNPARENCY

It's a see-through sun
that walks along and
sees through us so
glaringly, its see through
light too sleek a sprite
to pass through us but sparingly.
Our bodies stop its sunup
romp and reflect it back as
shadow. The night drops
and sunlight stops as
darkness curtains lower.
The stage is set for sleep and
dreams about which we must
ask: what sun is it that keeps
dreams lit throughout
our nightly task?

THE COOL SUN

For a thing so hot,
the sun is cool
to hang around
while lighting up
the ground. So hot
that we complain
without thanks for
its dance of shadows
whose coins collapse
in piles of chance
to liven up our lot.
Without the sun, we
would have never won
the time to be as cool
as the one that gives its sum
to me, to you, and the moon.

Made in the USA
Middletown, DE
03 June 2022